Cheng Man-Ch'ing

T'AI CHI CH'UAN

*A Simplified Method
of Calisthenics for
Health & Self Defense*

Cheng Man-ch'ing

North Atlantic Books
Berkeley, California

T'ai Chi Ch'uan
A Simplified Method of Calisthenic for Health & Self Defense

Copyright © 1981 by Juliana T. Cheng. All rights reserved. No portion of this book, except for brief review, may be reproduced, stored in a retrieval system, or transmitted in any form or by any means—electronic, mechanical, photocopying, recording, or otherwise—without written permission of the publisher.

Published by
North Atlantic Books
P.O. Box 12327
Berkeley, California 94712

Cover and book design by Paula Morrison
Typeset by Joe Safdie
Graphic production by Bill Tracy

Printed in the United States of America

T'ai Chi Ch'uan: A Simplified Method of Calisthenics for Health & Self Defense is sponsored by the Society for the Study of Native Arts and Sciences, a nonprofit educational corporation whose goals are to develop an educational and crosscultural perspective linking various scientific, social, and artistic fields; to nurture a holistic view of arts, sciences, humanities, and healing; and to publish and distribute literature on the relationship of mind, body, and nature.

Fifteenth Printing

TABLE OF CONTENTS

FOREWORD

After twenty years of concentrated effort, I published *Cheng's Thirteen Chapters on T'ai-chi Ch'uan* ten years ago. That book contains hardly one tenth of the valuable instruction and information on T'ai-chi Ch'uan and its underlying philosophy as handed down from the Sung Dynasty through Chang San-feng the Taoist, and as imparted to me by Professor Yang Cheng-fu: Yet many learners find the principles and theories expounded therein too difficult to understand. They have been plying me with all kinds of questions. For various reasons I have not been able to answer them more fully. Now, T'ai-chi Ch'uan is getting more popular and many people are trying to learn the right approach to it. Therefore I have no choice but to exert myself and write a simple text on this system of gymnastics in simple language and with diagrammatic illustrations for the benefit of beginners of either sex, old or young, in any state of health. To the thinking student, this book may serve as an introduction to the *Thirteen Chapters*.

In the *Thirteen Chapters*, the diagrams were taken from Professor Yang's notes and designed to illustrate the practicing of T'ai-chi Ch'uan in the form of boxing (as physical exercise and as an art of self-defence). Each exercise is performed by two novices, each of whom attacks and defends as circumstances require. The aim is twofold: to develop what is called the "body" of the art and to train for its application for pragmatic purposes. By the "body" is meant the movements and rhythm that make up the body of the art, and by its "application" is meant its usefulness from the points of view of health and self-defence. Since this double aim tends to confuse the beginner, this book will concern itself with teaching T'ai-chi Ch'uan as physical exercise rather than as an art of self-defence. The students may, therefore, practice singly, and the lessons and diagrams have been redesigned with this purpose in view. Very simple explanations help the students to understand the principles involved. It is further proposed to make use later of motion pictures to bring out the continuity and momentum of the movements, their speed and rhythm, their components and amplitude, etc., so as to remove any doubt or misunderstanding on the part of the beginners who depend on book instruction alone.

The most important point to remember is that one's *kung chia* must be in complete relaxation for success in T'ai-chi Ch'uan. *Kung chia* literally means "task framework," i.e., the "timber" of one's muscular disposition and flexing with the different parts of the body take up successive postures or execute successive movements. There should be no deliberate straining of the muscles. The old masters of this art used to say that "with a tense *kung chia,* even thirty years' practice will avail one of little. It will be useless as an art of self-defence, ineffectual as a form of physical exercise, and not be a way to rejuvenation." It behooves every novice to remind himself of this over and over, again and again.

Cheng Man-ch'ing
Taipei, August, 1956

N.B. In this and the following pages, parenthetical explanations enclosed in parentheses are the translator's.

This book contains only the fundamental exercises of T'ai-chi Ch'uan. In due course an advanced text will cover free hand operations (散手), pushing hands with active steps (活步推手), the art of using weapons, etc.

ACKNOWLEDGEMENTS

I owe my special thanks to many of my friends who have contributed to the compilation of this book. Dr. Hung Shih-hao, an old friend of mine, first embarked on the translation of this book some 30 years ago and finished only two chapters of it. Professor Cheng Cheng-yu continued the translation of another chapter 10 years ago. Both their efforts were later interrupted.

Dr. Hzu Tze-ming, another friend of mine, once mentioned to me that the terminology of this book was too profound and the book might have a wider reading public if more common expressions were used. Dr. Hsu, however, could not take part in the translation of it because he had a wrist injury at that time.

The present translation of my book was done through the joint efforts of Mr. Chang Chiu-shang, Dr. Hung Shih-hao, Mr. Hsu Tsu-jen, Col. Silo, Mr. C. K. Young, and Mrs. A. Young. The translated draft was revised by Dr. Beauson Tseng.

The sketches of the book with explanatory notes and the chapter on Pushing Hand Practice were rendered by Mr. Liang Tung-tsai and revised by Mr. R. W. Smith, Rev. Miss Ellen M. Studley, and Mr. Yu Hsien-wen. All the pictures in the book were taken by Mr. Kuo Ching-fang and Mr. Li Lee.

My appreciation is due to all my friends mentioned above through whose assistance the publication of this book is made possible.

Cheng Man-ch'ing

FOREWORD   George K. C. Yeh

T'ai-chi Ch'uan, as it is practiced in China today, is a system of physical exercise based on the principles of effortless breathing, rhythmic movement, and weight equilibrium. It is also designed to serve as a method of self-defense. As such, it can be practised by an individual alone in a limited space. It can also be practised by two opponents, one taking the offensive and the other defensive. It requires no equipment, except a loose-fitting garment which permits continuous rhythmic bodily movements. T'ai-chi Ch'uan has often been referred to, perhaps facetiously, by Westerners as "shadow boxing." When performed by an expert, its rhythmic movement reaches such a state of harmony that it can be likened to a form of dancing.

The essence of T'ai-chi Ch'uan lies in the maintenance of perfect body balance at all times. It illustrates most conclusively that in the case of any physical object, the larger its base and the lower its center of gravity, the greater is its stability. For this reason most of the movements of T'ai-chi Ch'uan are executed in a semi-crouch in order to achieve the maximum nature of stability, while offering the opponent the smallest possible target area. In this posture you are trained to attain the closest and nimblest coordination between the movement of the waist, the arm and the hand, and the movement of the legs in a series of continuous turns and shifts of footwork and bodily position. Of particular importance is the method of breathing required in these exercises which, I am told, gives the practitioner a continuous sense of relaxation so that he is never out of breath.

I am not a practitioner of the art myself, but I have heard and read much of the subtleties of T'ai-chi Ch'uan. An enthusiast could describe its effective employment as a means of bare-handed self-defense which would enable him to maneuver and triumph over a brutal assailant of superior prowess in a moment of emergency. I have personally witnessed a match between a T'ai-chi Ch'uan expert weighing about 120 pounds and a Western-trained boxer weighing at least 250 pounds, which ended in the boxer being thrown off his balance and brought to the ground.

One of the important aspects of the training is to learn how to avoid the impact of the onrush of the opponent's weight and to draw him into movements which will throw him off balance. The philosophy of T'ai-chi Ch'uan seems to echo the Taoist concept of "self-preserved" strength which comes from the perfect "inner control" of one's own physical posture. Its wisdom is found in the analogy that oaks may fall where reeds brave the storm.

It is generally agreed among historians that this form of self-defense was developed in the Sung Dynasty (960-1279 A.D.) by the famous boxer Chang San-feng, who was also the founder of the well-known Wu Tang school of boxing. Chang was a man of great physical strength and developed this form of rhythmic exercise as a corollary to boxing. There is no question that the present system of T'ai-chi Ch'uan has been elaborately extended from the simple movements originally developed by Chang San-feng.

Mr. Cheng Man-ch'ing, the author of this manual, has long been recognized as one of the foremost exponents of T'ai-chi Ch'uan in China. He is not only a T'ai-chi Ch'uan expert but also a poet, painter, and calligrapher. I have known him for over 30 years. Though I have not had the benefit of his instruction, many of my friends have and they regard him as an expert practitioner of the art as well as a successful instructor. I am very pleased that this manual, which has been widely used in China, has now been translated into English, and I would recommend it without reservation to anyone who desires to know more about this form of the boxing art which is as yet little known in the Western world.

George K. C. Yeh
Chinese Embassy
Washington, D.C.
January 26, 1961

FOREWORD   K. Schu

In a society as complicated as the present one, everyone, whatever his profession or vocation, will most probably feel his energy taxed past his endurance. It is therefore clear that unless a man is ready to retire from the world like a hermit in medieval times, his capacity to stand the daily strain without any means of recuperation must have a limit beyond which he can hardly carry on. Here is where the question of physical exercise comes in. Now in the West the term "physical exercise" includes various kinds of gymnastics, callisthenics, boxing, etc.—all designed to improve one's muscular grace and strength, or more rarely to defend oneself against unlooked-for violence. Perseverance in the practice of any of these arts would often reward the expert with results more than equal to his expectations.

In the East, especially in China, we also have experts who excel in one or more physical attainments enabling them to enjoy unusual health and longevity. But invaluable as such arts unquestionably are, few people realize their conduciveness to man's rejuvenescence. The adepts themselves, unless venally inclined, do not as a rule care to advertise for public notice as ordinary professionals often do.

Somewhat related to Chinese boxing, yet unique in character, is the so-called Metaphysical Boxing (T'ai-chi Ch'uan), discovered by the Taoist saint, Chang San-feng (between the 12th and 13th centuries). While practising mystical meditation in a state of semi-trance, he is said to have perceived how all parts of the human body act in unison to effect metabolism and facilitate blood circulation under the guidance of a vital principal. Repeated experience convinced him that instead of any artificial exercise as a means toward physical invigoration, one should rather follow or obey Nature in every movement of one's corporal organs, whether internal or external. That was why Chang finally came to put his personal experience together into a system. Thus not only his disciples but even laymen might profit by his unprecedented discovery if they would only persist in carrying out his instructions.

However, it must not be assumed that a tyro, once initiated

into the theory of this saintly art, could attain his end by sheer application of his own without further assistance. Constant advice from an expert is always necessary until the learner has become thoroughly acquainted with the procedural mode of operations in his daily exercise. Then he will often be surprised with some experience he did not expect in the beginning at all, such as a wonderful increase of staying power while tackling a piece of difficult work, a sudden cure of disease hitherto baffling to medical authorities, and the like.

But in spite of the numerous benefits Metaphysical Boxing could confer on a man if he would only submit to the training required of him, no one has so far undertaken to write an expository treatise thereon. Now the present author, Professor Cheng Man-ch'ing, has made up his mind to share the secret of this art with the whole world by publishing this rare good book. Here theory as well as practice is set forth in such lucid language that no misunderstanding of the text is possible.

However, lest the different forms of posture the learner ought to assume in his steady progress from one stage to another should not be entirely clear without illustrations, Professor Cheng has appended to the text a series of diagrams with explanatory notes. As far as its mode of exposition is concerned, this book may be said to be unrivalled in its kind. But to guarantee from disappointment, the student should never dispense with the service of an expert guide.

K. Schu
Professor of the Taiwan University

PREFACE   H. P. Tseng

My first contact with T'ai-chi Ch'uan, a form of old Chinese pugilistic art, dates back about 30 years. I was induced to learn it after a few of my friends had benefited from it, but I did not go through the whole course. For T'ai-chi Ch'uan comprises 128 movements. It takes considerable time to learn and it takes considerable time to practice. As a working newspaperman, I was busy and could find little time to follow a rigid program of daily exercise.

Then four years ago I met Professor Cheng Man-ch'ing. I heard that he had, for the convenience of beginners, reduced the number of movements to 37, by eliminating repetitions and preserving only the essential ones.

As my primary purpose was to improve my health, I have learned only the 37 movements, which I practice at home daily. I have never taken the advanced course of *t'ui shou* (推手), which teaches one the art of self-defense.

Gradually it has dawned on me that only by learning *t'ui shou* could one expect to have a deeper understanding of the significance of T'ai-chi Ch'uan. That is why I am still a beginner, although I have practiced T'ai-chi Ch'uan for four years without interruption.

Be that as it may, I have already benefited much from T'ai-chi Ch'uan. Considering my age, and I am 65, I must say that my health is exceptionally good. Before I learned T'ai-chi Ch'uan from Professor Cheng four years ago, I often suffered from rheumatism, a common ailent on Taiwan. I was also easily susceptible to colds. Furthermore, I easily felt tired and fatigued at the end of the day.

Now I am happy to say, all these troubles are gone. I feel as fit today as twenty years ago. This is no doubt a reward for practicing T'ai-chi Ch'uan regularly over a long period of time. I would like, therefore, to recommend this classic Chinese physical exercise to others.

Based upon my personal understanding, I wish to say a few words by way of introducing this art. The correct approach to T'ai-chi Ch'uan is spelt out in the 12 guiding principles which Professor Cheng had learned from his teacher Yang Cheng-fu, a

T'ai-chi Ch'uan authority in the early years of the Republic. Of the 12 principles *"sung"* (鬆 relax) and *"ch'en"* (沉 sink) are the most important ones.

The principle of *sung* is usually translated into English as *relax*. As it is difficult to find an equivalent in English to express the full and true meaning of *"sung"* as is understood by T'ai-chi Ch'uan experts, *relax* is about the closest word to it.

Ordinarily, *relax* means to give up energy. This, however, corresponds only to a part of the requirements under the principle of *"sung"*, which means loosening one's muscles and releasing one's pent-up tension.

But another phase of the same principle *"sung"* is that one should not give up his energy. Along with the related principle of *"ch'en"* (sink), *"sung"* requires that one should store up rather than give up his energy. Professor Yang said: "To relax completely means to sink." By this he meant that a student of T'ai-chi Ch'uan should not waste his energy purposelessly and meaninglessly, and instead, he should keep his energy in his *"tan t'ien"* (丹田) or the lower part of his abdomen. By doing so, one can give his whole body a chance to rest and at the same time conserve his energy.

A theory like this may sound strange to people in the West. But, Western medical research has discovered that anything wrong with one's nerve system automatically affects other parts of his body. It may interest them to know that T'ai-chi Ch'uan teaches one how to control his nervous system in order to put his whole body to rest.

It is a common experience that whenever we get excited, we feel tautness in our muscles, contraction in our hearts, and discomfort in our stomachs. To keep one's nerve system in a state of calm is one of the effective ways to keep healthy. Buddhists and Taoists who teach their disciples to sit for long hours in meditation follow the same principle. I venture to say that the principle of *"sung"* in T'ai-chi Ch'uan is to teach one how to achieve calmness in action and meditation in movement.

As to the principle of *"ch'en"*, it teaches one how to sink his *ch'i* (氣 breath) right down into his *tan t'ien*. It is basically a breathing exercise. According to T'ai-chi Ch'uan theoreticians, one should breathe deeply, slowly and quietly and let the *ch'i* (breath) sink to, and abide in, his *tan t'ien*.

Physiologically speaking, of course one breathes through his lungs, and so to breathe with one's abdomen is only a matter of feeling. Actually, it is still the lungs which do the breathing, but the abdomen muscles apply a pressure on the lungs to facilitate respiration. Consequently, the lungs assume a relatively passive role as they function under the pressure of the diaphragm which in turn is pressed by the abdomen muscles.

This kind of abdominal breathing provides one's internal organs with an opportunity of exercise. All Western physical exercises are limited to the movement of the external parts of one's body. T'ai-chi Ch'uan takes care of the internal organs as well. This is a contribution of major importance.

With regard to the self-defense part of T'ai-chi Ch'uan, I can only give a brief introduction based upon book knowledge and personal observation. As I have said before, the theory of *"sung"* is to store up rather than give up one's energy. In other words, it teaches one not to waste his energy without purpose but to concentrate and store it up for use in case of emergency.

One must not be tense before he can be alert. So long as one is alert, he can react rapidly and with ease whenever reaction is called for. Being alert gives one the feeling he could hear the movement of an attacker before the latter actually strikes. As one's energy is conserved, his reaction is bound to be quick and strong. This is my general impression whenever I watch Professor Cheng demonstrate his unmatchable skill in practicing *t'ui shou* with his students.

I am glad that Professor Cheng's masterpiece on T'ai-chi Ch'uan has been rendered into English and will soon become available to Western readers. It is my personal belief that T'ai-chi Ch'uan is an indispensable physical exercise for people who work constantly under tension.

Professor Yang Cheng-fu used to tell his students at least a dozen times a day: "Relax, relax and completely relax." This is a golden rule which every one living in these days of tension will do well to bear in mind.

H. P. Tseng
Director of Central News Agency of China

TRANSLATOR'S NOTE   Beauson Tseng

Mr. Cheng's treatment of his subject matter in this book is brief but comprehensive. The book will interest Western readers as a good example of how Chinese philosophy underlies Chinese art, or of how science in China is commingled with philosophy, no less than it will interest them as a self instructor of T'ai-chi Ch'uan. Chinese philosophy, particularly of the Taoist schools, is subtle and abstruse. In trying to make the translation intelligible to the average Western reader, I have added a few explanatory remarks. They are enclosed in parentheses. It is hoped that those who will use this book for its avowed purpose or for its philosophic side-lights will find the translation not too much off the mark. Criticism will be welcomed for revision purposes.

Beauson Tseng

PART I

T'ai-chi Diagram

（ 太極圖 ）

The T'ai-chi (Ultimate Principle of Existence) evolved the "Two Powers" (the white space represents yang; the black space represents yin) from which a coordinated and vigorous force is produced.

Chapter 1

T'AI CHI CH'UAN
AS PHYSICAL EXERCISE

The aim of practicing T'ai-chi Ch'uan as physical exercise is twofold: the substantive or that which aims at making up the "body" of the exercise; and the functional, or that which aims at securing its pragmatic value. The realization of this twofold aim depends upon six factors:

1. Course—how long has one been practicing?
2. Reach—how deeply has one reached out for what is most worthwhile achieving?
3. Kind—whether one exercises with rigid muscles in high-powered movements, or with pliable muscles almost effortlessly.
4. Adaptation—whether one is able to adapt principles to particular needs and thus to avoid slavish adherence to set form.
5. Skill—with what precision and ease one executes the movements of the body and the mind.
6. Understanding—how rapidly and clearly does one grasp the meaning and significance of the principles?

The above six factors depend in their turn upon three conditions: correct teaching, natural talent, and perseverance. Of the three, correct teaching (or right method) is of

1

primary importance. When the method is incorrect, or when the right method is wrongly taught, no success is attainable even if highly gifted or diligently and conscientiously applying oneself. On the other hand, given the right kind of teaching, even if one's natural talent should be below average, success can be achieved through perseverance. I shall, therefore, discuss the third condition first—for even the highly-gifted, correctly-instructed learner would be ruining his own chance of achievement should he fail to persevere. Indeed, it would be a waste of time to speak to him of learning *anything*.

Take my own case for example. When I was young, I was incurable in my lack of perseverance. Whenever my health was poorly, I practiced T'ai-chi Ch'uan. As soon as I felt better, I stopped. Thus it happened again and again. God be praised! For he did not want to give me up for lost and sent me illness after illness to oblige me to persevere in spite of my disinclination.

As I realized that I was lazy, I tried to find a way to make it easier for me to persevere. The kind of T'ai-chi Ch'uan that I had been taught comprises 128 movements, of which many are repetitions. To go through a full round takes more than ten minutes at the recommended speed. I tried to save time by hurrying it through at flying speed and succeeded in reducing the time to seven minutes—still too long to please me. Realizing that many others were facing the same difficulty, I decided to eliminate the repetitions and drastically to reduce the number of movements to 37. As compared with the earliest T'ai-chi Ch'uan of 13 movements, 37 is by no means a small number. The 37 movements, however, missed none of the constituent elements of the 128 and preserved the latter's original sequence as a system. To run through this simplified course takes from three to five minutes only, depending on one's speed. One round in the morning and one in the evening will total no more than ten minutes a day.

Usually I speak to my students thus: "For the sake of the nation or social order, or even for one's kith and kin, or neighbours, often one is prepared to dedicate one's whole life. How thoughtless it would be, therefore, to grudge oneself the ten-minutes-a-day-for-the-sake-of-physical-well-being!" Without sound health, as without education, what good can one do to one's nation or social order, kith and kin, or neighbours? None at all! One further point at this juncture: the daily exercise should be scheduled to have one round immediately after getting up, before the morning ablution; and the other immediately before going to bed for the night. The idea is, that whereas T'ai-chi Ch'uan banishes illness and poor health, food and sleep without exercise tend to breed them; and that whereas to skip a meal or a night's rest or two does not seriously matter, to skip a round of the daily exercise is highly undesirable. To be willing to be five minutes late for breakfast or bed time rather than miss a single round of the exercise is the way to insure perseverance.

As to the second condition, to be richly endowed with natural talent, is of course a great joy. Unfortunately, one cannot always count on nature's bountifulness; she is liberal to some and sparing to others. Moreover, once the allotment is made, it is fixed and unalterable, quite beyond human power to modify for the better. It is different with knowledge or skill,

3

both of which even the least talented may acquire through determined application. Speaking on the superior man and learning, Confucius says in *The Doctrine of the Mean* "... he will not intermit his labour. If another man succeeded by one effort, he will use a hundred efforts. If another man succeeded by ten efforts, he will use a thousand. Let a man proceed in this way, though dull, he will surely become intelligent; though weak, he will surely become strong." And he says again: "Some are born with knowledge ..., some ... by study; and some acquire the knowledge after a painful realization of their ignorance. But the knowledge being possessed, it comes to the same thing. Some practice them with a natural ease; some from a desire for their advantages; and some by strenuous effort. But the achievement being made, it comes to the same thing." Talent is not like this. Confucius once commented of his disciples, "Ch'ai is simple, Shen is dull." If Confucius' close associates were unequally endowed in natural talent, it is clear that natural talent cannot be counted on by the student of T'ai-chi Ch'uan. (Quotations taken from James Legge's translation of *The Four Books*.)

In regard to the first condition, namely, correct teaching or instruction, it is a subject far too profound for simple treatment. But I shall do my best. Everyone knows that as a result of different traditions of teaching and learning, philosophy as taught by Confucius and Mencius is sharply distinguishable from that by Yang Chu and Moh Ti. How important instruction is! But let us confine ourselves to the art of T'ai-chi Ch'uan. Classical verses like — "Having derived the quality of courage from the study of boxing, he is noted in history for his

4

muscular might" indicate that from very early times boxing was something associated with muscular might and physical courage. When Dharuma the Indian Buddhist (who arrived in China in the 6th c. A.D. and founded the Zen School of Buddhism) originated the Shao-lin school of boxing in Shaolin Temple, boxing was still conceived in terms of physical courage and muscular strength. It was well towards the end of Sung Dynasty (960-1278 A.D.) when a Taoist by the name of Chang San-feng first applied the philosophy of Huang Ti (Yellow Emperor, 27th c. B.C.) and Lao Tze to boxing, and substituted pliability for hard-hitting muscular power. This marked the beginning of T'ai-chi Ch'uan.

The Taoists constantly inquire: "Can you concentrate your *ch'i* and bring about a pliability like that of an infant'o?" From this idea, Chang derived his concept of the "body" of T'ai-chi Ch'uan. The Taoists speak of "the most pliable galloping the most powerful and unyielding as a horseman gallops his steed." From this, Chang derived another concept: that of the "function" or practical value of T'ai-chi Ch'uan—a concept exclusively based on the principle of "conquering the unyielding with the yielding." It is easy to perceive and understand how the courageous could defeat the timid, or the strong conquer the weak; but it is difficult to perceive or understand how the irresistible and unyielding could be overpowered by the pliable and yielding. One might cite from physical nature the example of brass being weathered away by gentle breezes or stone being bored through by dripping water. But the duration of time required to effect these changes render such examples poor illustrations. On the

5

other hand, a tornado is but the massed movement of air and a tidal wave that of water. As a whiff, nothing is more pliable than air; as a drop, nothing more yielding than water. But as tornadoes and tidal waves, air and water carry everything before them. Mass integration makes the difference. The entire weight of the galaxies of stars and universes do not rest on foundations more solid or weightier than they are themselves, but on the buoyancy of an immaterial "substance" referred to as *ether!* A similar kind of mental effort should enable us to perceive and understand the mass integration and mass movement of *ch'i* in Chang San-feng's theory.

T'ai-chi Ch'uan theoreticians speak of "the *ch'i* as sinking to, and abiding in, the *tan t'ien* or circulating throughout the body." They speak of the mind's "mobilizing the *ch'i*," or the *ch'i*'s "mobilizing the body," or of the *chi*'s "being gathered into the bones." At the highest level, they inquire if one's concentration of *ch'i* has brought one to the pliability of an infant. All these expressions refer to the derivation of power from *ch'i* through mass integration. The power thus derived is, like that of massed wind or water, simply immense. Its limit depends on the correctness of instruction and the amount of practice. May we never make light of the correctness of instruction! But the learner should realize that the primary purpose of such training is to enable him to achieve better physical health and emotional calm, and it is a matter of minor significance to train for self-defence or victory over others. All the talk about subduing "the unyielding with the yielding" stems from necessity rather than choice.

How, then, should a novice begin his training? The an-

6

swer is that he should relax. The relaxation should be overall, that is, throughout the entire body. And it should be thorough, that is, without the least strain anywhere. The aim is to throw every bone and muscle of the entire body wide open without hindrance or obstruction anywhere. When he has done this, he will be in a position to talk about *ch'i*. To start with, he should let his *ch'i* sink right down to the *tan t'ien*. To do this he should first relax his chest; for the *ch'i* can only sink freely when the chest is relaxed. Gradually, the *ch'i* will be felt to accumulate. Soon, it will be felt to circulate throughout the body. After that, the novice will be ready to direct the movement of the *ch'i* at will by means of his mind. This movement is technically known as a "propelled movement," for there is propulsion behind the movement just as an automobile or steamboat or aeroplane which does not move itself is moved by the gaseous power in the engine. In this sense, the limbs or other parts of the body during the exercises are moved not so much by means of local exertion or by expending local stores of muscular energy as by the force of *ch'i*. In other words, when we speak of "propelled movements" in T'ai-chi Ch'uan, we are not thinking so much of the stances and dances of the body or its parts as of something invisible, which we are mentally aware of as movements of the *ch'i*.

In the next, more advanced stage, the *ch'i* may be "occluded," i.e. absorbed and stored in the bones—causing the latter to become what is technically described as "*essentially* hard and indestructible." How can *ch'i* be occluded in a bone? This is not easy to explain, but I will try. Every piece of bone in a living person is seamless; and where bones join

7

together, they are connected by soft tendons or cartilages. When the *ch'i* has reached a certain stage of fullness as it accumulates in the *tan t'ien*, it begins to overflow. The overflowing *ch'i* is physiological, commonly known in China as *"hsueh ch'i,"* literally the *ch'i* of the blood. Overflowing the *tan t'ien*, this sanguinary *ch'i*, under the joint influence of the mind and the *ch'i* itself, accumulates and generates "heat" in the neighbourhood of the lower extremity of the spine. As a result, more *ch'i* is generated. When this stage is reached, the sanguinary *ch'i* may be directed to propel the *"ching ch'i"* (meaning the essence of life), causing the softer tendons and sinews, etc. to conduct the heat through the bone sheaths into the bones. The lower spinal vertebrae being thus heated up, the humour in them begins to "sweat", just as the wall of a test tube filled with warm air sweats on cooling. On cooling, the "sweat" congeals as marrow, tightly adhering to the inner pores of the bones. In time, the bones will be filled with this kind of marrow, which on repeated heating and cooling will consolidate into something hard, tough, and indestructible. When the *ch'i* has entered, and rendered the bones consolidated and indestructible, the learner has reached the highest level at which the "body" and the "function" of T'ai-chi Ch'uan can no longer be separated; they have attained unity. The bones are now indestructible, tough, and resilient, not brittle or weak, but as supple as an infant's! This is rejuvenation; at least the possibility of it. When one has achieved this advanced status of maturity in training or exercise, one has gone beyond the point of prolonging life and warding off disease. It is not pure nonsense that we speak of the extreme longevity of P'eng Ch'ien or Wu Hsien in Chinese legends.

Chapter 2

THE BODY
OF T'AI CHI CH'UAN:
ITS PRINCIPLES

The "propelled movements" of T'ai-chi Ch'uan aim primarily at exercising our internal organs. Man is the most spiritual among creatures. He is different from all other animals which do not hold themselves erect and which are less intelligent but more fierce or sturdy. One reason is that their internal organs are mostly suspended from a horizontal spine. The least movement of the animal exercises the whole set of its organs. Both the spine and the suspension muscles are strengthened thereby. Man sits, stands, and walks erect, thus allowing the lighter, purer (spiritual) elements in his body's make-up to rise high above the denser and the less pure. He is, therefore, endowed with a fuller measure of wisdom, and is distinct from animals by virtue of his spirituality. But the same cause also explains his inferiority in ferocity or brute strength. Both the spine and the internal organs of a human are vertically emplaced within a crowded space. The surfaces of the organs are contiguous and they suffer from the damp heat due to the close contact. The first organs to weaken under this action are the pancreas and the stomach; the next to yield are the lungs and the intestines; finally the rest of the vital organs. Poor health and sickness result therefrom. Even more important than the organs from the point of view of health is the

9

state of his spine which affects every part of his body. The weakening of the organs and their suspension muscles eventually weakens the spine itself—which is a condition never to be lightly overlooked by anyone who cares for his health. In the classics of T'ai-chi Ch'uan, it is said that:

> When the lowest vertebrae are plumb erect,
> The spirit reaches to the top of the head.
> With the top of the head as if suspended from above;
> The whole body feels itself light and nimble.

This is the main reason for exercising the spine. In order that the spirit rising up from the bottom of the spine—which is kept ram-rod straight and in a plumb erect position—to the very top of the head, it is particularly necessary that the head be held in a position as if suspended by the scalp from the roof or ceiling. This posture immobilizes the head and the spine so that neither could move up or down or sideways, and the spine is strengthened thereby. By strengthening the spine, one not only automatically strengthens one's vital organs but the brain itself. This is technically known as the effects or benefits of "replenishing or toning up the marrow."

In addition to the above, T'ai-chi Ch'uan classics speak of "allowing the *ch'i* to sink to the *tan t'ien*. *Tan t'ien* is a Taoist technical term which literally means the "field" for planting the *tan* (a gland-like product, conferring on the owner immortality and supernatural powers.) The position of *tan t'ien* in a person of average height may be determined as follows. Divide the horizontal line joining the navel and the spine in the ratio of 3:7, measuring from the former. The *tan*

10

t'ien is then situated at about 1 1/3 inches below the point of section. When the *ch'i* accumulates and develops vigorously in the *tan t'ien*, all "membranes" in the body will be strengthened, including the linings of the skin. As a tire is strengthened by air, so is the skin by the *ch'i*, with the membranes or linings of the skin playing the role of the rubber tube in the tire. A fully developed *tan t'ien* makes its owner's skin tough and resilient, able to resist wear and tear.

There are many other benefits. For example, by keeping the mind and *ch'i* in each other's "company" at *tan t'ien*, they can change the excessive water in the abdomen into *ch'i*. Abdominal contents are largely—about 70%—water. As a result many diseases stem from this aqueous excess. When there is enough *ch'i* in the *tan t'ien*, heat is generated which evaporates water. The evaporation not only diminishes the proportion of water but also keeps the circulation of blood and lymph. Another example: if the *ch'i* sinks to the *tan t'ien*, all the internal organs above the bulk of the intestines will reap the benefit of freer movement—expansion or contraction or vibration—which will mean countless blessings in terms of health. The more often one does this exercise, the greater will be the benefits. Be constantly on the alert to utilize any spare moments for keeping the mind and the *ch'i* in each other's company, which can be done when one walks, sits, or reclines, during travel by vehicle or on foot, or while waiting for trains or buses, or of course when deliberately resting, standing about, or lying down. Keeping the mind in the company of *ch'i* is much more invigorating than taking by mouth or by injection tonics or other forms of medication.

For those who can devote a few minutes in the morning, evening, or in some leisure hour for regular exercise, a few movements of what is called "dry swimming" in my *Thirteen Chapters* may be briefly described. Man lives on land; his long familiarity with air makes him often forgetful of its existence. Air is like water but has more uses. Since it lacks solidity and shape, it eludes attention or easy mental grasp by the beginner. To liken it to water aids imagination. After some time, he will realize that air is indeed like water in this sense: When one practices in air the movements of swimming as if he were in water, these movements would automatically conform to the principles of T'ai-chi Ch'uan. To look upon the latter as dry swimming is highly recommended for the novice, who may then convince himself of the likeness of air to water when he turns his palm, or waves his arm, in the breeze and feels its effect. Ultimately, he will "feel" the air to be heavier than water. By this time, he should know that his body and limbs are now lighter and more pliable than ordinary people's. This state of physical feeling of buoyancy and suppleness come from what is known as "firm rooting," with the soles "firmly cleaving to the ground." What I described elsewhere as "the spring-back to the upright by a lotus leaf in the breeze or by a weighted round-bottomed doll that cannot be pushed over," stems from this concept of dry swimming. The late President T'sai Chieh-min of National Peking University remarked thus: "T'ai-chi Ch'uan as an exercise spells self-defense and sound health, with everything to gain and nothing to lose. I should like to share it with my 400,000,000 compatriots. It is one of the highest of our national excellences." He voiced the truth.

Chapter 3

THE FUNCTION
OF T'AI CHI CH'UAN:
ITS PRINCIPLES

The application or function of T'ai-chi Ch'uan hinges entirely upon the player's consciousness. "To take advantage of impendence and momentum" and "to deflect the momentum of a thousand pounds with a trigger force of four ounces": are sayings which emphasize mental activities rather than physical force. Traditional boxing exalts physical bravery and muscular force with the addition of technique. Without physical bravery and force mere technique avails nothing. T'ai-chi Ch'uan holds a different view. T'ai-chi Ch'uan as an art of self-defense must completely spurn both physical bravery and muscular force. One is told that "in any action, the whole body must be made as light and free-moving as possible;" so light that "the addition of a feather will be felt for its weight, and so free-moving that a fly cannot alight on it without setting it in motion."

Besides the injunction to relax completely and not to exert muscular force, the novice is told "to give himself up and follow his opponent through." This is a caution that he must heed; otherwise, he will be doomed. Is it not ridiculous to speak of giving one's self up and following one's opponent through when one is resorting to boxing for, say, self-defense? When one is attacked with great force in a boxing duel, how can one give up and follow through as instructed? It seems incredible.

Yet this is actually so with one who practices T'ai-chi Ch'uan and has mastered its secrets. When his opponent directs a furious blow against him, he neither returns the blow nor withstands it. In fact, he receives no blow at all. Stepping aside, he merely takes advantage of the opponent's momentum and helps him with a push or pull, so that the augmented momentum, meeting with no resistance, will topple the agent himself to the ground. This is what is meant by taking possession of "impendence and momentum." This is how a mere four ounces may topple a thousand pounds. It does not mean that four ounces can overcome in direct opposition a force or moving mass of a thousand pounds, but merely to cause the latter to overcome itself. This technique stems from the idea of "giving up oneself and following the opponent through."

This is why I say that T'ai-chi Ch'uan is primarily concerned with physical culture. Its application as a means of self-defense is resorted to out of necessity only. A Confucianist sage will only employ military weapons when driven by necessity, not otherwise. T'ai-chi Ch'uan devotees have the same idea.

Relaxing the whole body by refusing to exert force or to tense one's muscles will ensure freedom of movement and deny the opponent of any chance of dealing a knock-out blow; for there is no center of gravity for him to act upon. Even this theory is but superficial. For deeper understanding, we must go to its source, the reasoning in T'ai-chi Ch'uan classics, which assert that sound boxing is "rooted in the feet," that it "sprouts (i.e., develops) in the legs," is "mastered or directed by the waist" and "moves up to or functions through the fingers." Since the *ch'i* moves up from what is known as the "bubbling well hsueh", to give "root" to the *ch'i*, one's feet must firmly cleave to the ground. By "sprouting the *ch'i*" in the legs is meant to develop the "spring" of them as a source of strength. That is to say, "strength is shot out of the legs as an arrow is from the bow". The waist may be likened to the bow that directs the arrow. Said philosopher Wang Young-ming (1472-1528) of Ming Dynasty: "Let the waist be as pliable as if it were boneless." He meant that the waist should be pliable, like an unstrung bowstring capable of being "doubled up a hundredfold without snapping asunder." The waist directs the strength just as the bow-string does the arrow and determines its direction, range, and penetrating power. For an arrow to hit the target, it must be correctly aimed and powered through the bow-string. So must T'ai-chi Ch'uan be directed by the waist. The *ch'i* is said to move up to the fingers because, as it wells up the legs, it will eventually reach the fingers. The force in an arrow reaches from the bow-string to the arrow tip. Likewise the *ch'i* in T'ai-chi Ch'uan reaches from the root—that is, from the feet—to the finger tips. This is what is meant by the phrase, "the application of T'ai-chi Ch'uan as boxing is rooted in the feet."

When experts speak of putting in efforts, literally "planting work," they mean planting exercises like planting seeds in the ground. When they speak of "growth work," they mean the upward development from the ground through the legs, just like a growing tree. And so, basically speaking, the state of complete, bodily relaxation has its roots in the feet. When a novice can so relax his body and "root" the boxing in his feet, the kind of boxing he is practicing is then technically termed the "internal physical culture" type of boxing. It refers to the kind symbolized by "the lotus leaf which sways but does not snap in the breeze," or by "the weighted doll which sways at the least touch but will not remain toppled however hit."

In practice, T'ai-chi Ch'uan is rooted in one foot at a time, never both simultaneously. Place all one's weight on one foot at a time so firmly that one feels oneself rooted in the ground like a tree with a single tap-root. To divide the weight on two feet is considered a serious mistake since the boxer will then lose agility due to the duplication of his center of gravity. This fault is technically known as "double weighting," which impedes instant readjustment of one's body posture.

When a tree is rooted in the ground, there is an actual root that penetrates the earth. When a boxer roots his foot in the ground, there is of course no material root, but the effect of rooting is nonetheless real. We all know the action of gravity. Well, in time, the T'ai-chi Ch'uan devotee, when he roots his foot in the ground, will feel as if his weight (force) has penetrated below the surface of the earth. The depth of penetration varies from a fraction of an inch to a foot or more. His concentrated force responds to gravity like iron to lodestone. This is known as "dropping to earth and taking root." How descriptive the phrase is!

Clearly, to speak of "the foot taking root" implies a concentration of physical force in the foot, leaving none in the rest of the body. When the body is entirely emptied of force a "tenacious strength" will develop from the foot. Tenacious strength may be distinguished from force in that the former has root while the latter has not. When in action, tenacity may be likened to a strong vine which is pliable, and force to a stick which is rigid. Hence we say: "tenacity is alive; force is inert." Tenacity is the resilience or tonicity of living muscles however relaxed they may be. The muscles being relaxed, tenacity cannot involve the bones. Force, on the other hand, is derived from the tension of muscles, binding the bones together into a wooden (rigid) system. Tradition has handed down, as a secret formula, that "tenacity is derived from muscles; force, from bones." To strike hard with force means the mobilization of all the bones and the tensing of all the muscles so that the blow may fall like a single mighty cudgel. To strike with tenacious strength involves no such mobilization or tensing; the blow falls like a pliable cane, with all one's bones at ease and resilient muscles in a state of complete relaxation. Being derived from muscles, tenacious strength is to be much preferred to brute force, because the strength is derived directly from the movements of one's *ch'i*.

Beginners find it difficult to distinguish tenacious strength from hard force. They should begin by practicing the *"t'ui shou"*, literally the pushing or outreaching hand as described in the diagrams. Only some theoretical points will be touched upon here. When two partners are practicing together, the *t'ui shou* is executed in the consciousness of four words: *chan, lien, t'ieh,* and *sui.* To *chan* is to adhere and lift (palms downward). To *lien* is to support and prevent from falling (palms upward). To *t'ieh* is to stick to horizontally. And to *sui* is to attach from the rear and not let go. The first two verbs have to do with up and down movements; the second two with to and fro and sidewise movements. The basic idea is light adherence: no letting go and no resistance. The partners keep their hands in continuous light touch while executing different movements. Each opponent is guided purely by the sense of touch which "detects" the other one's next move before it takes place. One yields at the partner's slightest pressure and sticks to him at his slightest retreat. One's palms are, so to speak, weightlessly glued to the partner's like a shadow to its object or an echo to the sound. Thus the exercises are gone through, over and over until one feels and anticipates almost by instinct the opponent's every movement, when one may be said to have arrived at the gate of mastering the "out-reaching hand." One is then ready for understanding the art of "interpreting strength." When one can so interpret, one has gone through the front gate and arrived at the parlor of T'ai-chi Ch'uan.

To interpret an opponent's strength is an art most difficult to explain. I shall present a rough idea only. T'ai-chi Ch'uan classics describe it as: "at the opponent's slightest stir, I have already anticipated it." It is similar to the military tactics of "starting after the enemy but arriving before he does." One learns to "detect the opponent's impending move, and then executes a counter-move before the enemy strikes." That is to say, wait until the enemy has committed himself to an intended move from which he cannot retreat; but as soon as this is done, one anticipates the enemy's actual move by moving likewise first. This is the basic principle of interpreting strength. Six kinds of tactics may be distinguished in boxing: the real or the feint; the solid (effective) or the hollow; the big or the little; the longer reach or the shorter; the rigid or the pliable; and the employment of "inner pliable strength" or "outer rigid force." They have to be nicely distinguished and interpreted. One can only acquire this ability to interpret by gradual improvement. But it all comes from developing a keen sense of touch.

At the highest level of interpretation, even the sense of touch is dispensed with. A T'ai-chi Ch'uan devotee of that perfection has his muscles, tendons, skin, and membranes so conditioned that they are automatically sensitive and alert, and will dodge a blow by reflex action even if he be attacked from behind without warning. It is a matter too difficult to explain here and the reader is referred to my *Thirteen Chapters*. He will then see how the function or practical application of T'ai-chi Ch'uan eventually attains this level. Yet it is within the reach of all, through correct instruction and regular practice. No special natural talent is necessary as a prerequisite. Any kind of boxing in which the stronger and the quicker in dealing out blows always defeats the weaker and the slower, may not be mentioned in the same breath with T'ai-chi Ch'uan as an art of self-defense.

Chapter 4

MY PERSONAL VIEW

Man cannot live healthily without taking exercises. The *Book of Change* says: "As nature is always in motion, so should man activate to strengthen himself without interruption." An ancient Chinese proverb says: "A door-pivot will never be worm-eaten and flowing water will never become putrid." All these aphorisms indicate that taking exercises leads to robust health. There are, however, many kinds of exercises from which one will have to make a choice. Some people exercise by lifting weights, some by wrestling. Others exercise by hiking, playing ball, skating, swimming, practicing traditional hard-hitting types of boxing, etc. Although these sports differ in form and scale, yet they have one thing in common, that is, they can never go beyond reliance on weight, force and the momentum due to speed.

Since this aspect has been dealt with in detail in the last chapter, I shall now confine my discussion to the differences in practice from various points of view. Exercises aiming at force and speed often cannot be taken under certain circumstances (e.g., when one's health is poorly). Traditional boxing and fencing are no exeption. It is also true of such exercises as hiking, weight-lifting. As for ball players, skaters, swimmers, etc., cold or sultry weather, heavy rains or scorching sunshine may keep them from regular practice. Moreover, some people are strong, others are frail; some are diligent, others are lazy; some are rich, others are poor; some are busy with their work, others have little to do. This accounts for the fact that different persons take exercises with different results. In some instances, taking exercises may do no good to one's health at all. In such cases, they have only themselves to blame for having chosen the wrong kind.

Now, T'ai-chi Ch'uan is without question a sport that suits everybody. In practicing it, the weak, the sick, the aged as well as children and women, will not find the draw-backs inseparable from exercises aiming at weight, force, or speed. Students and young folks will not be trained for bellicose purposes. No matter whether it shines or rains, no matter whether one be rich or poor, busy or leisurely, T'ai-chi Ch'uan can be practiced without such danger as one faces in skating or swimming, and without such toil and moil as one finds in weight-lifting, wrestling, fencing, or conventional boxing. So long as one has three feet square of space and can spare seven minutes a day, one can practice it without expending a penny. Taking this kind of exercise alone or together with others, alike will bring about lasting health and joy.

Among all kinds of sports, T'ai-chi Ch'uan is probably the easiest, the most convenient and the most economical to enable one to banish weak health or worry. It is hoped that those who know that taking exercise is indispensable to health will choose T'ai-chi Ch'uan. Personally, I think it is especially appropriate for women. The physical condition of woman is powerfully influenced by the condition of her blood. Irregular menstruation foreshadows illness. As blood is normally tranquil, so to speak, too strenuous activity for a woman will adversely affect her circulation. Just as boiling soup is liable to dry up quickly, so will menstruation become irregular (for the overactive).

From the Sung Dynasty to about fifty years ago, propriety and custom imposed too much restraint on women and the consequences on women's health have certainly been undesirable. After women's emancipation movements got under way at the beginning of the Republic of China, all restraints previously imposed on women have been quickly removed. Nowadays, a woman not only allows her feet and breasts to grow to their natural size, but also dresses differently from formerly, exposing her shoulders, chest, and legs to a considerable extent. Such sports as running, swimming, high jumping, ball-playing, etc., have been practiced by almost every young woman. Women are now often active in social service. But too much activity for a woman tends to overstimulate her physical metabolism. So far as a woman's health is concerned, taking too drastic exercises is as bad as taking no exercise.

The health of a nation depends on the health of its women. Healthy mothers usually give birth to healthy babies while unhealthy mothers to unhealthy ones. Like sowing seeds, fertilized soil yields rich crops while barren soil poor ones. Since taking exercises is so important to women's health, it is most advisable for them to adopt T'ai-chi Ch'uan.

In practicing T'ai-chi Ch'uan, one's body and limbs must be poised and balanced. The poised posture, balanced movements, easy and relaxed muscles as advocated in this book are in perfect agreement with the theory of centre of gravity of the human body. It should be pointed out again that the movements of T'ai-chi Ch'uan have a lot to do with one's spine. It conforms with a principle of physiology that certain sympathetic nerves take charge of the consumption, and certain other sympathetic nerves take charge of the replenishment, of bodily vitality. As this is treated in detail in my *Thirteen Chapters* on T'ai-chi Ch'uan, I shall go no further here.

In short, physical exercises should be taken in conformity with the criteria of natural poise, mildness, relaxation, and comfort. If there are other wonderful methods of physical exercise which can equally benefit human beings, I have to hold my tongue. I do not know of any.

Chapter 5

MY HOPE

The Taoists advocate *wu wei*, and the Buddhists venerate the doctrine of emptying. He who is dedicated to non-action seeks to realize the great hope of immortality. He who endeavors to empty the world of objectivity does so to cultivate his spirit which is his only real self. Similarly, I would adopt as my watchword for T'ai-chi Ch'uan the simple phrase, "investment in loss" — for a devotee voluntarily and at his own initiative to suffer "loss" will gain for him the benefit of health. To be more explicit, he who invests in small losses makes small gains, and he who invests in bigger losses makes bigger gains. Both the Taoists and the Buddhists in their doctrines aim at the salvation of people's souls, but, first of all, they must save their own. To invest in loss is the same as what Confucius meant by *k'e ch'i*, to subdue the self. Mencius says in his book, "When Heaven is about to confer a great office on any man, it first exercises his mind with suffering and his sinews and bones with toil, . . . exposes his body to hunger, . . . and supplies his incompetencies." The basic commandment of the Confucian doctrine is for one to subdue the self and to seek *jen*—i.e., to develop in one the virtues of love, creativity, and harmony; and then to extend one's self to others, i.e., to enlarge one's sphere of goodness by helping other people to do good. Although I

24

have not risen to the height of Confucius' teaching, I try to learn and to venerate its meaning and spirit. In advocating voluntary investment in losses, I am hoping that my fellow countrymen may reap the benefits of supplying their incompetencies and thus to clear from us Chinese the undignified appellation of the "infirm people of the Far East."

But, what is the first step for us to take toward investing in losses? According to what I have read originally it meant to yield oneself to follow other people, but it has often been mistaken for giving up the accessible for the inaccessible. If one can yield oneself to follow other people, one will have no stubbornness of any kind—"no foregone conclusions, no arbitrary determinations, no obstinacy, and no egotism." This is not far from the concept of "subduing the self."

When a novice practices T'ai-chi Ch'uan as a form of boxing with an "opponent," he is told to yield himself to follow through the opponent's movements. But as soon as he stretches out his palms, he may immediately lose the bout by being pulled down or pushed over by the opponent. If he is not ready to suffer such losses, how can he learn to yield himself to follow through the movements of the other man. The method of following the other's movements is to follow them in direction, high or low, advancing or retreating, forwards or backwards: without anticipation, without deliberately assuming any ensuing movement of the opponent's as being inevitable. Such yielding movement cannot be executed by anyone whose mind is obstinate and whose ego dominates. When with perseverance a person takes a yielding attitude and is able to suffer great losses so as to get his incompetencies

25

CHENG MAN-CH'ING

supplied as taught by Mencius, he has the hope of great success in any achievement, and therefore in physical exercise. By practicing the principles of yielding oneself to follow through other's ways and of suffering losses, one approaches the idea of "subduing the self", one of the highest virtues in Confucian doctrine. At what higher level can one aim?

To learn to suffer losses, however, is not an easy thing. On hearing that T'ai-chi Ch'uan is sound both in its make-up and its function, people often want to learn it with a view to picking up a bargain, not to suffering losses. My advocacy of suffering losses is, therefore, both difficult to understand and difficult to practice. Hence I cannot but stress my point here. No one has ever profited from any undue benefit without paying for it in the form of unexpected or inexorable losses. Small benefits bring about small losses and big benefits big losses. This is common knowledge. Yet when I make use of it in the reverse, some people are skeptical. They have not applied their mind to the problem. For example, good position and luxurious living may be considered benefits, but one has to pay for them in health. The reason is: these benefits are only superficial; he has not earned them by strenuous toil as farmers or gardeners have theirs. To put it in another way, those accustomed to a life of wine, women, and song are seemingly favored with good fortune. Yet in the end they may be troubled with diseases. They are not nearly as fortunate as a Taoist hermit or a Buddhist monk who enjoys none of these. So, in worldly affairs, it is often the one who seeks benefits that suffers losses. The pity is these people are intoxicated in sensual enjoyments and do not sober up. These are only a few

26

examples from many.

To gain benefits is not very difficult, but it is hard to seek losses. Benefits gained through losses hurt no one and may bring about unexpected advantages to the sufferer. It is much better than the benefits intentionally sought or struggled for. What is the benefit of learning T'ai-chi Ch'uan? Duelling by boxing is often a dangerous practice, because neither party is sure to win; both parties may suffer injury. At the worse — well, need one speak about it? We can see no benefit from it. And so to learn how to suffer losses begins with yielding oneself to follow through other's movements. This will cultivate in him what is known as the ability to "listen to strength" which is what has been treated in a previous chapter on "function." To be able to listen to other people's strength is the sure way to win, almost 100% sure, because it is the method of "using the yielding to overcome the unyielding." Consider the unyielding teeth and the yielding tongue, it is the tongue that outlasts the teeth. Students have to learn this principle through careful thought and clear observation. My reason for advocating T'ai-chi Ch'uan in this book is to help people to do good and to extend what one values oneself to others. In order to attain this objective, the primary requirement is to invest in losses from the beginning to the end. Would it not be a tremendous boon if any personal sacrifice could procure some universal benefit for all mankind!

Chapter 6

MY OWN EXPERIENCE

I seldom agree or disagree easily with other people. I try to hold fast to the right and the true of facts and theories. A deaf man knows no difference of sound, a blind man knows no difference of color, — because their respective sensory organ is out of order. To agree or disagree easily with others is analogous to a deaf man or a blind man, accepting what he is told without the equipment for independent judgment. In discussing T'ai-chi Ch'uan, I do not expect others to agree easily with me. I do not claim that I have cultivated the virtue of being able to extend myself to others or of helping people to do good. I only try to do so. I shall do my best to publicize my limited practical experience for the sake of my fellow countrymen. My own family and my students can testify to my sincerity and I do not say things which belie my heart.

In my younger days when I was teaching in the Yu Wen University and the College of Beaux Arts in Peking, my health was extraordinarily poor. I forced myself to stay there for five years. In the summer of 1925 I returned to Shanghai and reluctantly accepted teaching posts at the Shanghai College of Arts and Chi-Nan University. Later I founded the Chinese Arts College there. In a few years my tuberculosis became so bad that I almost succumbed. My relatives and friends found no way to help me. Shortly afterwards, I was introduced to Professor Yang by a Mr. Pu to learn T'ai-chi Ch'uan. Within a few months the internal hemmorrhage ceased and my temperature returned to normal. In less than a year my coughing was gone. In six or seven years other symptoms such as headache, loose teeth, dim eyesight and failure of concentration all disappeared. Now in my 55th year of age I can do everything anyone else is normally able to do. My eyesight has improved, to a state even better than it was thirty years ago, and my teeth are as good as in my younger days. I can walk a hundred *li* or do some stiff mountain-climbing with ease. As to the practical uses I have made of this art and how it has improved my sleep and appetite, they are described in detail in my *Thirteen Chapters* and will not be repeated here.

A man's life is limited whereas the calls made upon it are not. If he finds no way to get strong such as by the cultivation of the *hao jan chih ch'i* (the spirit which pervades and fulfills a person and the universe as advocated by Mencius), little hope has he of harvesting in full the benefits of health. The untimely death of a man like *Yen Yuen* (a disciple of Confucius) or Chu Ke-Liang (d. 3rd. c. A.D., one of China's greatest statesmen) signifies not only a personal loss but also a national calamity. The ups and downs of the Great Tao (the Way) concerns the welfare of a nation. The truth of this is beyond the power of words to explain even one part in ten thousand. Let no one belittle it!

PART II

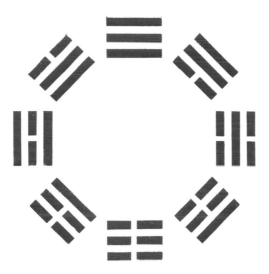

The Eight Trigrams

（八　卦）

The action of "ward off," "roll back," "press,"
"push," "pull," "chop," "elbowing" and
"shouldering" in T'ai-chi Ch'uan coincide
with the functions of evolution and operations of nature in the Eight Diagrams.

A SIMPLIFIED EXPLANATION OF T'AI-CHI CH'UAN

FIGURE 1   PREPARATION.

Stand erect facing north. Shift your weight to your right leg, bend it slightly, and rest on it. Pick up your left foot, take a step laterally to the left (west), and rest on it. Now raise your right toes slightly and turn your right foot on the heel inwards at 45° until it is parallel with your left foot, toes of both feet pointing straight ahead. The distance between your feet should be equal to that between your shoulders. In this position your elbows should be bent slightly outward with the backs of your wrists curved upward. Your palms are down and the tips of your fingers raised slightly and relaxed, neither tightly stretched nor clenched. Your head is erect and your eyes look straight ahead. Your shoulders and elbows are loose and your chest depressed, thus enabling your *"ch'i"* to sink to your *tan t'ien* (a point just below the navel. See explanation in Chapter One). Your tongue should be held against the upper palate and your mouth and lips tightly closed. Your mind is at ease and concentrates tranquilly on your breathing.

預
備
式

1   PREPARATION.

(Yu Pei Shih).

FIGURE 2   BEGINNING.

Inhaling slowly, raise your arms with the wrists bent upward to shoulder height. When they reach this level mobilize your *ch'i* and extend your fingers. Now draw back your arms by bending your elbows and again relax your fingers. When your hands are near your chest, lightly take them to your side, your wrists carried as though sinking into water and your fingertips floating off. Now you are again in the posture ending Figure 1.

起
勢

2 BEGINNING.

(Ch'i Shih).

FIGURE 3A   GRASP THE SPARROW'S TAIL (WARD OFF WITH YOUR LEFT HAND).

Shifting your weight to your left leg, relax the right side of your upper torso and turn on your right heel, toes slightly raised to the direct right (east). Your right foot is now at right angles to your left foot. In turning you must move your waist and thigh simultaneously with your foot. At the same time bring your right hand, palm down, to the level of your armpits, and your left hand, palm up, parallel with your right thigh. Thus you simulate holding a ball in your hands. Your eyes follow this movement and now look directly to the right. Now shift your weight to your right leg.

攬雀尾左掤

3A GRASP THE SPARROW'S TAIL (WARD OFF WITH YOUR LEFT HAND).

(Lan Chueh Wei, Tso P'eng).

FIGURE 3B   GRASP THE SPARROW'S TAIL (WARD OFF WITH YOUR LEFT HAND).

Your left foot is brought to toes and then take a step directly north with your left foot, the heel touching first. Bending your left knee, you shift your weight to the left foot gradually while turning the right side of your upper torso to the left. Bring your left hand up to a point parallel with your chest, palm toward you and elbow slightly down. Simultaneously drop your right hand beside your right thigh. It is important that your eyes follow the gradual turn and look directly north when the turn is completed by the final movement—a slight turn of your right foot on your heel so that the toe is slightly inward.

攬雀尾左掤

3B GRASP THE SPARROW'S TAIL (WARD OFF WITH YOUR LEFT HAND).

(Lan Chueh Wei, Tso P'eng).

FIGURE 4   GRASP THE SPARROW'S TAIL (WARD OFF WITH YOUR RIGHT HAND)

Shift more of your weight to your left leg until your right foot is brought to toes. Simultaneously turn your left hand over so that the palm is down while the palm of your right hand is up. Relaxing your left shoulder, turn your right thigh to the right and turn on your right toes about 45° placing your right foot down heel first just an inch or so forward of its previous position. Shift your weight from your left leg to your bent right leg. Protect with your right arm, elbow down, palm toward your chest, and your left arm, elbow down, the palm forward midway between the right wrist and elbow but not touching. Stretch the left leg and turn the foot slightly inward. You now face directly to the east.

攬雀尾右掤

4 **GRASP THE SPARROW'S TAIL (WARD OFF WITH YOUR RIGHT HAND)**

(Lan Ch'ueh Wei, Yu P'eng).

FIGURE 5   GRASP THE SPARROW'S TAIL (ROLL BACK).

Relax your right arm and turn your upper torso to the right (southeast). Turn your right wrist to the northeast while your left hand, palm up, is held near your right elbow for protection. Then bend your left knee and turn your upper torso and arms back to the left (northwest).

攬雀尾擺

 5   **GRASP THE SPARROW'S TAIL (ROLL BACK).**

(Lan Ch'ueh Wei, Lu).

FIGURE 6   GRASP THE SPARROW'S TAIL (PRESS).

Continuing, carry your left hand in a circle, turn your right hand so the palm is facing your chest and protect with your right arm, elbow bent, while the fingers of your left hand lightly attach your right arm between the elbow and wrist. Stretch your left leg and shift your weight to your right leg. Press diagonally upward. You are now facing directly east again.

攬雀尾擠

 GRASP THE SPARROW'S TAIL (PRESS).

(Lan Ch'ueh Wei, Chi).

FIGURE 7 GRASP THE SPARROW'S TAIL (PUSH).

Shift your weight again to your left foot while separating your hands with the palms facing away from your body. Then shift your weight forward to your right leg and push forward with both hands and upper torso. Your elbows should be bent but your arms must not act independently of your body. Your arms move only in conjunction with your body.

攬雀尾按

7 GRASP THE SPARROW'S TAIL (PUSH).

(Lan Ch'ueh Wei, An).

FIGURE 8   SINGLE WHIP.

Shift your weight to your left foot, turn on your right heel, and holding your arms parallel and slightly bent at the elbows, turn your body as far as it will go to the backward left corner. Now shift your weight to your right leg. Bring your left palm up near your right armpit and bringing your right hand across your chest join the fingers together, pointing downward, to resemble a hook. Simultaneously, raise your left heel and turn the foot slightly to the right with the entire leg while extending your right "hook hand" to the right corner (northeast), relaxed and not rigid. Now take a big step to the forward left with your left foot, the heel touching the ground first. Shift your weight to the left leg and bend the knee. At the same time your left hand, palm inward, is carried at chest level to the left until your waist faces due west. Now your right toe is turned with your right knee inward (in order to straighten your waist) and your left palm is turned outward as your eyes follow the turn and look along the fingers of your extended left hand.

8   SINGLE WHIP.

(Tan Pien).

FIGURE 9   LIFTING THE HANDS.

Turn your upper torso slightly to the right and shift your weight to your left leg. Resting on your left leg, bring your right foot to the right side front and put your right heel down lightly, toes up and knee bent. Relax your arms and turn them inward so that your palms face. Slowly bring your arms closer together until your right palm is in front, aligned with your right leg, and your left palm in back by your left ribs and directly opposite your right elbow. The backs of your wrists are slightly bowed.

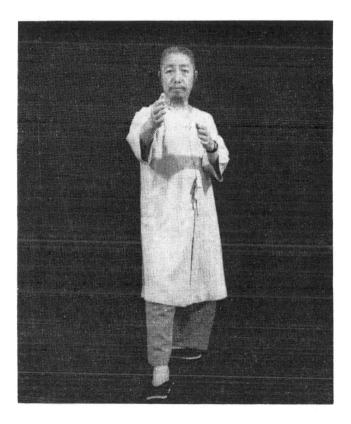

提手

9 LIFTING THE HANDS.

(T'i Shou).

FIGURE 10   LEAN FORWARD.

Now bring your left and right arms and your right leg simultaneously back: your left hand hangs down beside your left thigh; your right hand, palm inward, is near your abdomen; and your right toes touch the ground near your left heel. Next, take one step forward with your right foot and shift your weight to that leg. Your right hand protects your groin and your left hand is held near the middle of your right forearm. Your right shoulder leans slightly forward as you continue to face north.

靠

10 LEAN FORWARD.

(K'ao).

FIGURE 11 THE CRANE SPREADS ITS WINGS.

Turn your body to the left (west) and at the same time raise your right arm in a small circle inside your left and carry it up to where your right elbow nearly parallels your chin and your right hand stretches over your head. Simultaneously, put your left hand down beside your left thigh. Bring your left foot forward diagonally right and put the toe down at a point on a line with your right heel.

白
鶴
亮
翅

11 THE CRANE SPREADS ITS WINGS.

(Pai Hao Liang Ch'ih).

CHENG MAN-CH'ING

FIGURE 12   BRUSH LEFT KNEE AND TWIST STEP.

Lower your body while your weight is still on your right foot. Turn slightly to your right and lower your right hand beside your right thigh while your left hand circles clockwise past your chest and stops by your right thigh. Take one step with your left foot to the diagonal forward left, heel touching first. Simultaneously, circle your right hand from the rear up past your right ear and brush your left knee with your left hand (palm down), stopping it by your left knee. Your weight will have shifted during this movement and now rests on your left leg. You still face west.

56

左
摟
膝
抝
步

12 BRUSH LEFT KNEE AND TWIST STEP.

(Tso Lou Hsih Yao Pu).

CHENG MAN-CH'ING

FIGURE 13 PLAYING THE GUITAR.

Pick up your right foot, turn it 30° to the right, and shift your weight to it. While bringing your right hand back with the palm toward you, raise your left hand so that the fingers are in front of your nose. Your right hand should now be opposite your left elbow. At the same time, your left foot takes a half-step directly to the right, only your heel touching the ground. This position simulates playing a guitar.

BRUSH LEFT KNEE AND TWIST STEP.

(Tso Lou Hsih Yao Pu).

Repeat the instructions given for Figure 12.

58

手揮琵琶

13 PLAYING THE GUITAR.

(Shou Hui P'i Pa).

FIGURE 14   STEP FORWARD, DEFLECT DOWNWARD, INTERCEPT AND PUNCH.

Withdraw and lower your body and place your right palm beside your left thigh. Turn on the left heel, put your toes down 3 inches to the left, and rest on it. Simultaneously, raise your right foot and take a half-step to the diagonal forward right to where the toes point northeast, and shift your weight to it. Make a fist with your right hand and carry it, knuckles down, to rest under your right ribs. At the same time your left hand circles up beside your left ear and chops forward. Next your left foot steps forward, heel touching first.

進步搬攔捶

14 STEP FORWARD, DEFLECT DOWNWARD, INTERCEPT AND PUNCH.

(Chin Pu, Pan Lan Ch'ui).

FIGURE 15   STEP FORWARD, DEFLECT DOWNWARD, INTERCEPT AND PUNCH.

The weight is shifted to the left foot. Your right fist follows the movement of your waist and left leg and strikes forward from underneath your left palm and wrist. Your chop and punch must be delivered slowly and gracefully without force.

進步搬攔捶

15 STEP FORWARD, DEFLECT DOWNWARD, INTERCEPT AND PUNCH.

(Chin Pu, Pan Lan Ch'ui).

FIGURE 16   WITHDRAW AND PUSH.

Open your right fist and bring it back close to your left shoulder. Simultaneously, your weight shifts rearward to your right leg. Your left arm is brought up outside your right and both palms face your chest, thus forming a slanting cross shape. Bring them even further back near your chest, separate your hands turning the palms out and push forward (as in Figure 7). At the same time your weight shifts to your left leg.

如
封
似
閉

16 WITHDRAW AND PUSH.

(Ju Feng Szu Pi).

FIGURE 17A   CROSSING HANDS.

Now shift your weight to your right leg and turn your body to the right (north) with your right arm carried in a high circle and your left arm following your waist. At the same time turn on your left heel so that your foot bends inward facing north.

十字手

17A CROSSING HANDS.

(Shih Tzu Shou).

FIGURE 17B   CROSSING HANDS.

Next shift your weight to your left leg. Your left hand should describe a smaller circle than your right and both should end up before your chest in a diagonal cross, your right arm outside your left. Simultaneously, draw your right foot to the rear toward your left foot until the two feet are aligned to your shoulders (as in Figure 2 except that now all of your weight is on your left foot rather than distributed on both).

十字手

17B CROSSING HANDS.

(Shih Tzu Shou).

FIGURE 18   EMBRACE THE TIGER TO RETURN TO THE MOUNTAIN.

Turn your waist to the right rear (southeast) and simultaneously separate your hands, the right palm down and the left palm up. As your left hand descends turn it to the left rear. Take one step with your right foot to the right rear (southeast) and shift your weight to it. Your right hand next brushes your right knee and then is turned so that the palm is up. At the same time stretch your left hand palm down to the right (southeast) and look directly over it. Finally, turn on your left heel so that your foot is slightly inward and aligned to the direction you face.

GRASP THE SPARROW'S TAIL, ROLL BACK, PRESS AND PUSH.

(Lan Ch'ueh Wei, Lu, Chi, An).

The explanations of the above postures are the same as before.

SLANTING SINGLE WHIP.

(Shieh Tan Pien).

The explanation is the same as for Figure 8, "Single Whip," the only difference being that in the last step of "Slanting Single Whip" you face northwest while on the "Single Whip" you face west.

70

抱虎歸山

18 EMBRACE THE TIGER TO RETURN TO THE MOUNTAIN.

(Pao Hu Kuei Shan).

FIGURE 19   LOOKING AT THE FIST UNDER THE ELBOW.

Lower your body and draw back. With your left foot take one step to the left side (west) and shift your weight to it. At the same time open your right "hook" hand, turn your upper torso to the left, and bring your right foot forward, your toes pointing northwest and on a line with your left heel. Shifting your weight to your right leg, continue turning your upper torso left with both your arms evenly stretched. When you have turned as far as you can and your right hand is opposite your left shoulder, your left hand circles from underneath your left armpit, and is held, fingers pointing up, almost perpendicularly before you. At the same time take one-half step with your left foot diagonally to the front center, only the heel touching, and make a fist with your right hand and bring it up to where it cups your left elbow.

肘底看捶

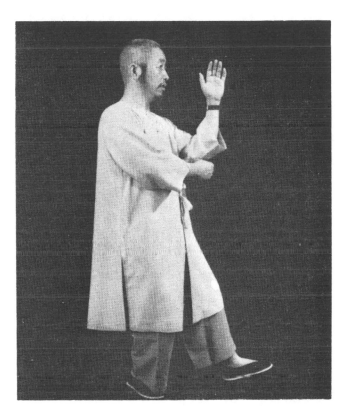

19 LOOKING AT THE FIST UNDER THE ELBOW.

(Chou Ti Kan Ch'ui).

FIGURE 20 STEP BACK TO DRIVE THE MONKEY AWAY (RIGHT STYLE).

Open your right fist and draw it back, palm up, to your right side. Turn your left hand palm down and extend the arm to the front. At the same time step slightly diagonally to your left rear with your left foot and place it down so that it is exactly straight (pointing west). Shifting your weight to your left foot, turn your right toe inward so that both feet are parallel. Now turn your left hand, palm up, and draw it back by your left thigh, while your right hand circles backward and turns so that the palm is down. The fingers of your right hand then pass your right ear and pierce directly forward.

倒
攆
猴
右

20 STEP BACK TO DRIVE THE MONKEY AWAY (RIGHT STYLE).

(Tao Nien Hou Y'u).

FIGURE 21   STEP BACK TO DRIVE THE MONKEY AWAY, LEFT AND RIGHT STYLES.

The explanations of the above styles are the same as before.

倒
攆
猴
左

21 **STEP BACK TO DRIVE THE MONKEY AWAY,
LEFT AND RIGHT STYLES**

(Tao Nien Hou, Ts'o Shih, Y'u Shih).

CHENG MAN-CH'ING

FIGURE 22   DIAGONAL FLYING POSTURE.

Turn your right palm up and put your hand beside your left thigh. Turn your left palm down at the same time so that your hands simulate holding a ball. Take one step with your right foot to the right rear (northeast) and shift your weight to it. At the same time circle your right arm under your left armpit to your right rear where it is extended palm up. Turn on your left heel 45° to the right, your waist accompanying the move, and lightly hold your left hand palm near your right knee.

斜飛勢

22 DIAGONAL FLYING POSTURE.

(Hsieh Fei Shih).

FIGURE 23A   WAVING HANDS IN THE CLOUDS, RIGHT STYLE.

Turn your right hand palm down and draw it back to your right armpit. While turning your upper torso to the right as much as you can, turn your left hand, palm up, beside your right thigh and under your right hand. Again your hands simulate holding a ball. Now take one-half step forward to the north with your left foot. Circle your right hand, palm in, under your left, and begin turning your upper torso toward your left, while your right foot takes one-half step to the left, toes directly frontal so that both feet are parallel. Thus the position of your feet is now the same as in Figure 2 (Beginning). Carrying your left hand, palm in, at the level of your throat and your right hand at the level of your navel continue turning to your left until your hands again simulate holding a ball by the left side, left hand above. Throughout the movement your upper torso should be erect and not inclined to either side.

右雲手

23A WAVING HANDS IN THE CLOUDS, RIGHT STYLE.

(Y'u Yun Shou).

CHENG MAN-CH'ING

23B WAVING HANDS IN THE CLOUDS, LEFT STYLE.

(Ts'o Yun Shou).

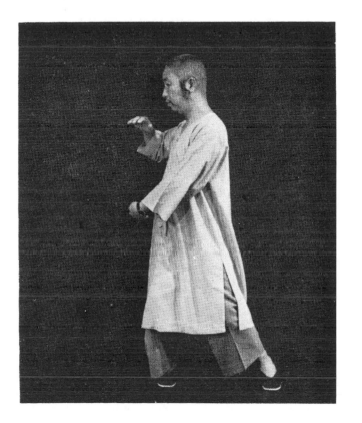

右雲手

24 WAVING HANDS IN THE CLOUDS, RIGHT STYLE, LEFT STYLE AND SINGLE WHIP.

(Y'u Yun Shou, Ts'o Yun Shou, Tan Pien).

The explanations of the above three styles are the same as before.

FIGURE 25   SINGLE WHIP SQUATTING DOWN.

Turn your right foot on its heel 45° to the right as you draw back and lower your body so that you almost sit on your right foot. Curve your left foot 45° inward to the right and draw back your left hand to your right thigh, then thrust it down along the left knee and heel and forward. Turn on your left heel 90° to the left as your left hand thrusts forward. Your right hand is kept hooked to help maintain stability.

單鞭下勢

25 SINGLE WHIP SQUATTING DOWN.

(Tan Pien Hsia Shih).

FIGURE 26   THE GOLDEN PHEASANT STANDS ON ONE LEG.

As your left hand is thrust forward your body rises. Bend your left leg slightly and shift your weight to it. Turn your right foot on the heel 45° to the left. At the same time drop your right hand beside your right thigh and open the hooked hand. Immediately raise your right hand and right leg, bent at the knee, so that your toes point down. Your left hand lightly touches your left thigh.

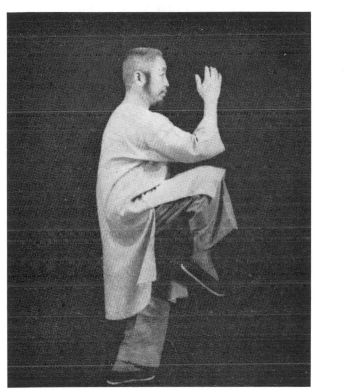

金鷄獨立右式

26 THE GOLDEN PHEASANT STANDS ON ONE LEG.

(Chin Chi Tu Li Shih).

FIGURE 27   THE GOLDEN PHEASANT STANDS ON ONE LEG, LEFT STYLE.

The explanations are the same as for Figure 26 except that your hands and feet are changed alternately.

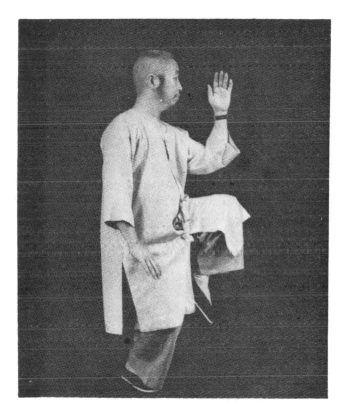

金鷄獨立左式

27 THE GOLDEN PHEASANT STANDS ON ONE LEG, LEFT STYLE.

(Chin Chi Tu Li Tso Shih).

CHENG MAN-CH'ING

FIGURE 28   SEPARATE THE RIGHT FOOT.

Lower your body, take one step to the rear left (southeast) with your left foot, and shift your weight to it. Simultaneously turn your left hand, palm up, and lower it while you turn to the southeast. Raising your right hand, palm in, to neck level, stretch it forward, palm down, and then bring it back toward your chest. At the same time your left hand is turned, palm down and circles clockwise to where it joins your right wrist in a "slanting cross" shape in front of your chest. Separate your hands in the opposite direction while simultaneously kicking your right foot forward. Keep your right foot straight with the instep and your right hand aligned to your right foot. The flash of your eyes and your right hand are focused on the intended object. Your left arm has the elbow bent and fingers pointing upward so as to maintain balance.

90

右分脚

28 SEPARATE THE RIGHT FOOT.

(Y'u Fen Chio).

FIGURE 29   SEPARATE THE LEFT FOOT.

The explanations are the same as before except that your two feet are changed alternately.

左分脚

29 SEPARATE THE LEFT FOOT.

(Tso Fen Chio).

FIGURE 30   TURN AROUND AND STRIKE WITH HEEL.

Withdraw your left hand and left foot. Raising the right toes slightly, turn on your right heel to the left with the toes facing south and the upper torso facing east. Your right hand circles counter-clockwise where it joins the left wrist. Your left foot kicks out while your left hand chops directly forward (east) and your right hand slightly back, fingers pointing up to sustain balance. This kick is different from the preceding ones in that the heel is used rather than the toes as the striking member. Your right leg should be bent and your eyes focused over your left fingers.

BRUSH THE LEFT KNEE, BRUSH THE RIGHT KNEE.

(Tso Yu Lou Hsi).

The explanations of these two movements are the same as before.

轉身蹬脚

30 TURN AROUND AND STRIKE WITH HEEL.

(Chuan Shen Teng Chio).

FIGURE 31   STEP FORWARD AND STRIKE WITH FIST.

Relax your waist and shift your weight to your left leg. Turn the toes of your right foot to the right, make a fist with your right hand and hold it, palm up, by your right thigh. At the same time draw your left palm back beside your right thigh and shift your weight to your right leg. Now take one step forward with your left leg and shift your weight to it. Then brush your left knee with your left hand and hold it by your side while your right fist strikes forward on a descending line.

STEP FORWARD AND WARD OFF.

(Shang Pu P'eng).

Shifting your weight to your right foot, turn the toes of your left foot lightly to your left. Now shift your weight to this foot. Open your right fist and ward off forward. Take a step forward with your right foot. The explanations of the sequence which follows, "Roll Back," "Press," "Push" and "Single Whip" have been given previously.

進步栽捶

31 STEP FORWARD AND STRIKE WITH FIST.

(Chin Pu Tsai Ch'ui).

FIGURE 32   THE FAIRY WEAVING AT THE SHUTTLE (1).

Draw your body back and shift your weight to your right leg, turn on the heel of your left foot as far as you can to the right and shift your weight to it. Your body accompanies the left foot in turning right and now you face northeast. Draw back your left hand and put it under your right armpit. Opening your right "hook hand," turn the palm outward. Draw your right foot back slightly and shift your weight to it. Now take a full step to the northeast with your left foot and shift your weight to it. At the same time slide your left hand, palm in, up along your right forearm, and then turn it outward. It is now stretched across your forehead for protection. Press your right palm forward in a pushing motion while your right knee is stretched slightly to add impetus.

玉
女
穿
梭
(一)

32 THE FAIRY WEAVING AT THE SHUTTLE (1).

(Yu Nu Ch'uan Suo (1)).

FIGURE 33   THE FAIRY WEAVING AT THE SHUTTLE (2).

Draw your body back, turn your left toes inward to the right as far as you can. Turn your right palm up and put it under your left elbow. Now turn your body 180° to the right, taking a long step further right with your right foot. Your right foot should now point northwest. Bend your right leg and shift your weight to it. The remainder of this action is the same as in the previous figure.

玉女穿梭（二）

33 THE FAIRY WEAVING AT THE SHUTTLE (2).

(Yu Nu Ch'uan Suo (2)).

THE FAIRY WEAVING AT THE SHUTTLE (3).

(Yu Nu Ch'uan Suo (3)).

Draw back your body, shift your weight to your left foot. Now turn your left palm up, put it under your right elbow, and shift your weight to your right leg. Turn 90° to the left (southwest) and take one step forward with your left foot. The remainder of this action is the same as in the previous two figures.

THE FAIRY WEAVING AT THE SHUTTLE (4).

(Yü Nu Ch'uen Suo (4)).

Draw back your body, shift your weight to your right leg. At the same time turn your left toes inward to the right as far as you can. Shifting your weight back to your left foot, turn your body 270° to the right (southeast) and take one step forward with your right foot. The remainder of this action is the same as in the previous three figures.

GRASP THE SPARROW'S TAIL, WARD OFF, ROLL BACK, PRESS, PUSH AND SINGLE WHIP SQUATTING DOWN

(Lan Ch'ueh Wei, P'eng, Lu, Chi, An, Tan Pien Hsia Shih)

These actions are performed exactly as described previously.

FIGURE 34 STEP FORWARD TO THE SEVEN STARS OF
THE DIPPER.

As your body rises, shift your weight to your left foot. Take one-half step forward with your right foot, only the toes touching the ground. No weight is put on the foot. Open your right "hook hand" and carry it forward with the right foot. When it is in front of your chest clench both hands into fists and join them at the wrists, the left hand inside, the right hand outside.

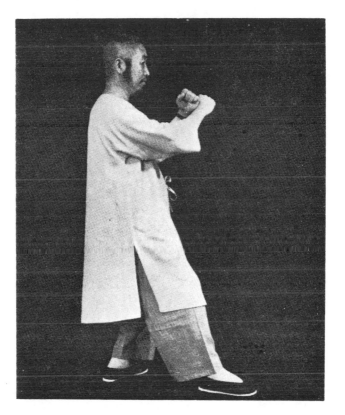

上步七星

34 STEP FORWARD TO THE SEVEN STARS OF THE DIPPER.

(Shang Pu Ch'i Hsing).

FIGURE 35   STEP BACK TO RIDE THE TIGER.

Draw back your right leg one full step and shift your weight to it. Now take one-half step back with your left foot, only your toes touching the ground. At the same time your fists are opened and your right hand circles right and is held beside your right shoulder, the forearm vertical, the fingers up, and the palm outward. After opening your left fist, brush it over your left knee.

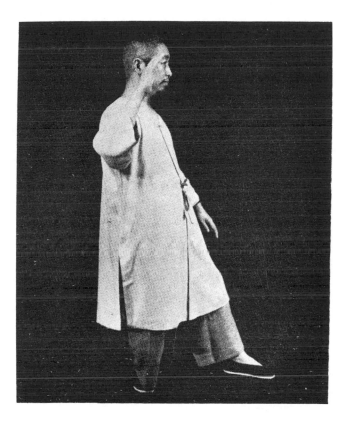

退步跨虎

35 **STEP BACK TO RIDE THE TIGER.**

(T'ui Pu K'ua Hu).

FIGURE 36   TURNING THE BODY TO SWEEP THE LOTUS WITH THE LEG.

Stretching your left arm further to your left, circle your right hand to your left waist. While your left heel is raised, raise your right heel slightly and turn your body a complete 360° turn to the right, your weight remaining on your right foot. Your right foot is still on its toes. Your two arms are slightly extended forward and aligned to your shoulders. Now shift your weight to the left leg and raise your right leg in a circle and carry it from left to right horizontally, slightly touching your two palms.

轉身擺蓮腿

36 TURNING THE BODY TO SWEEP THE LOTUS WITH THE LEG.

(Chuan Shen Pai Lien T'ui).

FIGURE 37 BEND THE BOW TO SHOOT THE TIGER.

Lower your right foot so that it points northwest. Move both hands simultaneously, the right palm out, left palm in, toward your right side. When your right hand reaches your right ear, the left hand is directly ahead of your left chest, and at this time both hands are made into fists. The spaces between the thumb and index finger of each hand face each other.

STEP FORWARD, DEFLECT DOWNWARD, INTERCEPT AND PUNCH, WITHDRAW AND PUSH, AND CROSSING HANDS.

(Chin Pu Pan Lan Ch'ui, Ju Feng Szu Pi, Shih Tzu Shou).

The explanations of the above postures are the same as before.

CONCLUSION OF T'AI CHI.

(Ho T'ai Chi).

Relax and open your hands and lower to the side of the thighs. Following the dropping of the hands the legs are straightened as in Figure 2, "Beginning".

110

彎弓射虎

37 BEND THE BOW TO SHOOT THE TIGER.

(Wan Kung She Hu).

PUSHING HAND PRACTICE WITH FIXED STEPS

Pushing hand practice *(t'ui shou)* is the next step in learning T'ai-chi Ch'uan. It is practiced by two players standing facing each other. The basic movements are "ward off," "roll back," "press" and "push" — all included in the "Grasp the Sparrow's Tail." The following principles must be incorporated into the practice or it will not be successful.

1. Relax and yield to your opponent.
2. The players are in constant touch as they execute the movements.
3. Be guided by "feel"; detect your opponent's move before he begins.
4. No resistance, every response should be a gentle one.
5. In the context of the four movements making up this exercise there are four actions which must be distinguished.

   a. To adhere and lift — palm down (chan)
   b. To join — palm up (lien)

c. To adhere horizontally (t'ieh)
d. To attach from the rear (sui)
a and b are up and down movements; c and d are backward, forward and lateral movements. For details refer to Chapter 3.

After much practice three stages are possible; (1) the opponent's energy is "heard" before it is used, (2) the energy is "interpreted" before it is used, and—the summit of T'ai-chi Ch'uan—(3) complete mastery of an opponent is had without recourse to detecting his energy.

The following figures illustrate Pushing Hand Practice with Fixed Steps. For clarity the players are termed A (the Author, with Whiskers) and B (the translator).

FIGURE 1   SINGLE HAND MOVEMENT

A faces B at a distance of about three feet. A takes a step forward with his left foot, raises his left forearm to his chest with the palm in, and approaches it between B's left elbow and wrist. The weight is focused on the left leg and the left forearm is kept relaxed. A's right hand rests lightly beside his right thigh. B's actions are the same as A's. By moving with one hand up and down, to and fro, and right and left the players will detect the energy of the four moves (1) adhere and lift (chan), (2) join (lien), (3) stick to horizontally (t'ieh), and (4) attach from the rear (sui). This exercise is called "single hand movement" and is a preliminary exercise to the movements employing both hands which follow.

1 SINGLE HAND MOVEMENT.

FIGURE 2   WARD OFF (P'ENG).

A steps back one pace with his left foot and steps forward with his right. His right forearm is raised before his chest, palm inward, and B's forearm adheres to it. The left hand of both players is held between the chest and right elbow, palm outward. The weight rests on the right leg. This is called "right ward off." Ward off is not used to attack your opponent, but rather is guided by the sense of touch which detects his move so that you may turn your waist, nullify his attack, and thus use four ounces of energy to defeat him.

掤

2   WARD OFF (P'ENG).

FIGURE 3   PRESS (CHI).

When A uses "ward off" to attack, B uses "adhere and lift" and returns ready to attack. A then puts his left palm in the middle of his right forearm, shifts his entire weight to his right leg, and with the momentum of his lower torso presses forward against B's chest. If B neutralizes this press, A should stop short or he will be unbalanced forward. If B does not or cannot neutralize and uses strength, A will use "adhere and lift" and "press" to unearth B.

3   **PRESS (CHI).**

FIGURE 4   ROLL BACK (LU).

If A's "press" is neutralized he will turn his waist to the right rear, lower his right elbow, then circle counter-clockwise with his right arm until the right elbow touches B's left elbow. The back of A's left wrist adheres to B's left "push hand," palm in, and as B pushes the palm is turned slightly up. This coupled with a slight overturning of the right elbow neutralizes B's push in A's left rear. The left palm should not touch A's chest but is held close to it. The action of the left and right arms, relaxed but efficient, combined with a shifting of the weight to the left leg, is indeed subtle. It is literally "capturing the enemy after leading him into ambush."

攦

4   ROLL BACK (LU).

FIGURE 5   PUSH (AN).

When A rolls back, B must stop his push or unbalance himself. A then places his right palm on the rear of B's wrist and his left palm on B's right elbow. Looking directly forward, A pushes with the momentum transmitted from his lower torso and B is pushed over. If the push is done incorrectly, the fault may rest with one of these reasons: (1) A has not detected B's faulty move correctly or has acted on it too late; (2) A has pushed without having a postural advantage, and thus he opposes strength with strength; and (3) A has neither detected B's defective move nor utilized a postural advantage. Students should observe clearly and think carefully on these basic moves. Otherwise progress in T'ai-chi Ch'uan will not come.

按

5   PUSH (AN).

THE ESSENTIALS OF PUSHING HAND PRACTICE

1. When your opponent strikes you with strength, instead of opposing him (force against force), you simply withdraw your body, neutralizing his weight—thus his weight will be emptied and will not come to your body.

2. When attacking your opponent you should not attack him immediately. Your hands first must lightly touch his body and as soon as you interpret that he is going to resist you, you yield (withdraw) slightly and then immediately attack (withdraw-attack techniques).

3. When interpreting your opponent's energy you should not put too much weight against him during the time of interpretation. A T'ai-chi Ch'uan devotee when performing "pushing hand practice" must follow the above mentioned principles strictly so that his art progresses rapidly —otherwise, he will be doomed.

At the highest level the T'ai-chi Ch'uan devotee can arrive at a stage of what is technically called the application of "receiving energy." "Receiving energy" is entirely different from force against force. When your opponent attacks you with a rubber ball you may use a little force to knock the ball and bounce it away. This is force against force and is not "receiving energy." Suppose your opponent attacks you with an iron ball of 500 pounds, can you also use a little force to bounce it away like that of a rubber ball? The correct application of "receiving energy" is that when the ball comes near to your body you first have to attract it like iron to a lodestone and then throw it out. The degree of velocity and the amount of weight you have used must be very accurate. The interpreting, sticking, withdrawing and attacking energies are all involved in an instant. This is the reason why T'ai-chi Ch'uan surpasses all other forms of boxing from the standpoint of practical value.

HOW TO UPROOT
YOUR OPPONENT

When engaging in "pushing hand practice" the most efficient way of attacking is to "up-root" both feet of your opponent. If you can only "up-root" his front foot your method of "withdraw-attack" is not correct. To realize this the following 6 factors are important:

1. T'ai-chi Ch'uan theoreticians say that sound boxing is rooted in the foot, that it sprouts in the legs, is directed by the waist, and moves up to and functions through the fingers. The feet, the legs, and the waist must move as one. Before attacking you must withdraw slightly, turn the waist upright, and use the tenacious energy (energy from the sinews) instead of the hard force (force from the bones of the body). When attacking you should have the concept of pushing slightly upward. The tenacious energy is shifted from your hind leg to your front leg from where it is directed into the ground. Your front knee is bent and should not extend over the tiptoes of the foot, otherwise your energy will be dispersed. Your shoulders and elbows should be loose. The lowest vertebra is to be plumb erect and the head should be upright. When you have done all these things your tenacious energy will be unified and can break down any strong point of your

opponent. Lacking any of the above mentioned essentials, your strength can not be concentrated and your efficiency will be greatly decreased.

2. When both of your hands touch your opponent's body before attacking, you should not use too much force; otherwise you will give him a chance to interpret you and as soon as you start to attack him he can neutralize your weight slightly and you will fail to "up-root" him.

3. When your hands lightly touch him you have to detect a slight wave of resistance in his body. By taking the advantage of this wave, you will be able to attack him decisively. It is rather difficult to detect the wave in a person. If you do "pushing hand practice" over a long period you will find it.

4. When attacking you should not use force with both of your hands. T'ai-chi Ch'uan classics say that when attacking it is necessary to aim at one direction of your opponent. To use force with both of your hands is technically known as double weighting and contradicts the principles of T'ai-chi Ch'uan. The correct way is to use one hand while the other hand simply touches the opponent's body without any effort.

5. The position of your hands and arms to your body before attacking should remain the same as after attacking. The disproportionate stretching and shrinking of the hands and arms when attacking will effect the unified action of the tenacious energy from your leg and the

efficacy of the "up-root" will be greatly decreased.

6. When attacking you have to withdraw slightly with the concept of going downward first and then going up so that you can "up-root" your opponent. T'ai-chi Ch'uan classics say that if you want to push upward you must first go downward. For instance, if you want to pull something up you have to push down first and the root will be naturally broken off.

The following diagrams indicate how to "up-root" your opponent with the techniques of "pushing hand practise." The first diagram is to "up-root" by applying the technique of "ward off," the second diagram is to "up-root" by applying the technique of "press," and the third one is to "up-root" by applying the technique of "push." All these techniques are included in the "pushing hand practise."

捌

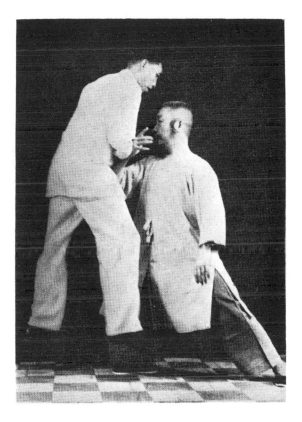

First diagram.   **"WARD OFF" "UP-ROOT"**

Second diagram.   **"PRESS" "UP-ROOT"**

按

Third diagram.   **"PUSH" "UP-ROOT"**

CHENG MAN-CH'ING

SOME EVENTS IN THE LIVES OF THE YANG FAMILY

When my teacher's grandfather, Yang Lu-ch'an (楊露禪), first walked into the Palace during the Ch'ing Dynasty he was attacked by two dogs who bit his legs and then, with strange barks fled. Mr. Yang paid no heed and followed the eunuchs with a quiet smile. The eunuchs were amazed at his non-chalance. Later it was learned that the dogs, who refused to eat that night, had left some broken teeth at the place the attack occurred—so strong were Yang's legs.

•   •   •   •   •

Another time my teacher's eldest uncle Yang Pan-hou (楊班侯)—the eldest son of Yang Lu-ch'an—was napping one summer evening in the yard while awaiting dinner. A servant nudged him to announce that dinner was ready and Yang, still sound asleep, kicked the poor fellow nearly to the level of the roof.

•   •   •   •   •

One morning my teacher's father, Yang Chien-hou (楊健侯), the third son of Yang Lu-ch'an, was approached by a servant who told him that a dead rat was stuck on the bedroom wall. Did the master know anything about it? Yang thought and then said: "It must have been that the rat tried to get at the peanuts in my pocket while I slept. I must have caught him and thrown him at the wall with such force that he stuck."

.   .   .   .   .

One rainy day about 30 years ago my teacher, Yang Ch'eng-fu (楊澄甫), grandson of Yang Lu-ch'an, and I were crossing the Outer Paitu Bridge in Shanghai. A large sturdy man walking very quickly ran smack into Yang and promptly recoiled several feet onto his back. He arose and stared angrily at the quiet Yang but, apparently so surprised that he had failed to move him, walked away without speaking.

.   .   .   .   .

I, Man-ch'ing, evaluate these four instances as illustrative of actions done without conscious effort. T'ai-chi Ch'uan classics say that when one understands the "interpreting energy"—one is gradually arriving in the parlor of the supernatural.

THE SOLO EXERCISE

1. Stand at Attention.
2. Preparation.
3. Beginning
4. Grasp the Sparrow's Tail (Left Ward Off, Right Ward Off, Roll Back, Press, Push).
5. Single Whip.
6. Lifting the Hands.
7. Lean Forward.
8. The Crane Spreads its Wings.
9. Brush Knee and Twist Step.
10. Playing the Guitar.
11. Brush Knee and Twist Step.
12. Step Forward, Deflect Downward, Intercept and Punch.
13. Withdraw and Push.
14. Crossing Hands.
15. Embrace the Tinger to Return to the Mountain.
16. Grasp the Sparrow's Tail.
17. Slanting Single Whip.
18. Looking at the Fist Under the Elbow.

19. Step Back to Drive the Monkey Away.
20. Diagonal Flying Postures.
21. Waving Hands in the Clouds.
22. Single Whip.
23. Single Whip Squatting.
24. The Golden Pheasant Stands on One Leg.
25. Separate the Left and Right Feet.
26. Turn Around and Strike with Heel.
27. Brush the Knee.
28. Step Forward and Strike with Fist.
29. Grasp the Sparrow's Tail.
30. Single Whip.
31. The Fairy Weaving at the Shuttle.
32. Grasp the Sparrow's Tail.
33. Single Whip.
34. Single Whip Squatting Down.
35. Step Forward to the Seven Stars of the Dipper.
36. Step Back to Ride the Tiger.
37. Turning the Body to Sweep the Lotus with the Leg.
38. Bend the Bow to Shoot the Tiger.
39. Step Forward, Deflect Downward, Intercept and Punch.
40. Withdraw and Push.
41. Crossing Hands.
42. Conclusion of T'ai-chi.

**T'ai-chi and Eight Trigrams
United in One**

（ 太極八卦配合圖 ）